The Great Skate RACE

By Tisha Hamilton
Illustrated by Jackie Urbanovic

Modern Curriculum Press

Computer colorizations by Jacki Hasko

Cover and book design by Lisa Ann Arcuri

ISBN 0-7652-1373-7

Printed in the United States of America

8 9 10 11 12   07 06

1-800-321-3106
www.pearsonlearning.com

Contents

**To my two Williams,
everything is possible**

1

Get Ready

The big day was finally here. It was the day of the Ridge City Skate Race. All the animals were excited. They had been getting ready for the race all year. Many racers came from far away to skate in this famous race.

Molly Mouse could barely see the starting line. She was the smallest skater. Molly really wanted to win this race. Everyone thought she was too small to win. Molly believed she could win.

Happy Hippo was ready to race, too. He was the biggest skater. He planned to get in front right away. Then none of the other skaters would be able to get around him.

START

Lazy Gator thought she could win, too.
She had almost won last year. Tabby Cat had
gotten ahead of her on the last turn.

Rocky Raccoon and Pinky Pig tried to find
a spot away from Lazy Gator. Last year they
both had been knocked down by Lazy's tail.

Ozzie Ostrich was just happy to be at the
race. She would be racing for the first time.

The skaters looked at their race maps one more time. They checked where the signs would be that would tell them where to go.

Then a whistle blew for the racers to line up. The race was about to begin!

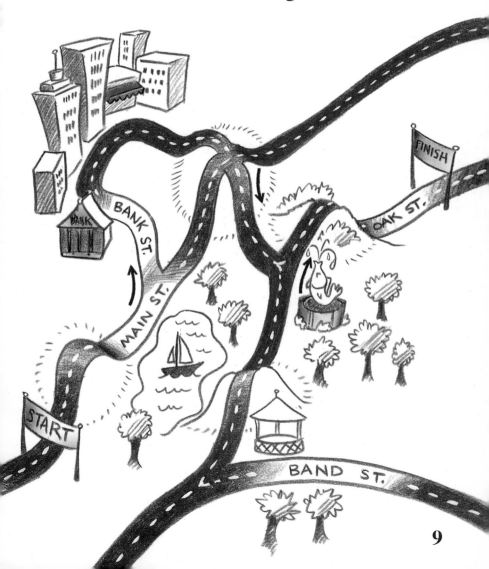

Chapter 2
On Your Mark

The skaters lined up. Chip raised the starting flag. The crowd held its breath. Then the whistle blew again. The flag came down. The skaters took off.

Happy Hippo's left skate hit the road.
Thump! His right skate hit the road. Thump!
His strong legs pushed. Faster and faster he
skated down Main Street. He was winning!

Happy skated past Sailboat Pond. He waved to the sailors. The sailors waved back.

As Happy raised his arm to wave he slowed down. Tabby Cat saw his chance. He skated around Happy. Now Tabby was in front.

Happy was surprised. He pushed harder and tried to catch up to Tabby. Suddenly Happy's skate hit the curb. Happy wobbled off the road. The other skaters raced passed him.

On the road ahead was a sign. On the sign
was an arrow that pointed left. Tabby Cat
turned left and raced by the First Animal
Savings Bank. He was still in front, but the
other skaters were close behind.

Tabby Cat made a wide turn around the next corner. He was skating fast. Then suddenly he was flying up into the air.

Tabby had skated up some long boards. They were lying against the back of a truck. Tabby landed on a pile of sand. He wasn't hurt, but he was dizzy. Lazy Gator chuckled as she skated by. Now she was winning!

A Shortcut

Rocky Raccoon and Pinky Pig tried hard to catch up to Lazy Gator. They felt bad when they saw Tabby sitting on the sand. They were going too fast to stop.

Molly Mouse was the last skater to come around the corner. She saw Tabby sitting on the sand.

"I should stop," she thought. "If I stop, I'll never catch up. What should I do?"

Molly had to stop and help Tabby. "You can do it, Tabby," she said. "Keep skating."

"Thanks," Tabby said.

Around the next corner, Rocky and Pinky were right behind Lazy Gator. They were skating hard. They forgot about her tail. Swish, swish! Lazy Gator swung her tail.

Rocky and Pinky tried to get out of the way. The tail was too big. The tail knocked Pinky into a bush. Rocky flew into a trash bin.

Lazy Gator skated on into Posey Park. "No one can catch me now," she said.

Fish Fountain was just ahead. A sign in front of the fountain pointed left. Lazy Gator stopped and looked. The path went up a steep hill.

"Skating uphill is hard," Lazy said. "The other skaters might catch up to me."

Lazy thought and thought. Then she had an idea. Quickly she turned the sign. The arrow now pointed right. Lazy Gator laughed as she skated up the path to the left.

Which Way?

Molly and Tabby were skating toward the park when they heard sounds. Molly stopped.

"What was that noise?" she thought. She saw Pinky stuck in a bush. She heard Rocky in a trash bin. "I have to help," she said. So she stopped.

Molly helped Pinky out of the bush. She
helped Rocky out of the trash bin.

"Thanks," Pinky and Rocky said.

"Let's go," Molly said. "We can still catch
up to the other skaters."

Molly, Pinky, and Rocky skated into the park. Just ahead they could see Fish Fountain and most of the skaters. They were all turning right.

"Wait, that's the wrong way," Molly yelled. It was too late.

"The sign points to the right," Rocky said.

"The map says to go left," Molly said. She opened her map and showed them.

SKATE
RACE

"You go to the left," Molly said to Pinky and Rocky. "I'll try to catch up to the others." She turned right and started skating down the hill.

"Am I too late?" Molly thought. She pumped her legs faster and faster. She almost flew along.

The skaters raced down the hill. The hill became steeper and steeper. The skaters went faster and faster.

Ozzie Ostrich was in front. She thought she was winning. She skated faster. Then she looked ahead. At the bottom of the hill was a street. On the street was a big parade with a marching band. The skaters would never be able to stop.

All the skaters rolled right into the band. Ozzie ducked under a tuba. A dog whirled around a drummer. A squirrel just missed hitting a horn player. Molly skated right into the middle of everything.

"Go back," Molly yelled. "You went the wrong way!"

Finally the skaters stopped. They turned and started back up the hill. Molly followed as best she could. The other skaters were soon far ahead.

"I will never win this race," Molly thought, "but I will finish it." She skated even harder.

5

A Mice Surprise

Molly was very tired, but she kept skating. At last she saw the finish line ahead. "Everyone else must have finished a long time ago," she thought.

The crowd cheered as she crossed the finish line.

"Why are they cheering?" wondered Molly. "I didn't win."

Molly could see Lazy Gator up ahead. She was holding a big silver trophy. She wasn't smiling.

"Lazy Gator must have won," Molly thought. "I wonder why she looks so unhappy."

Lazy Gator skated up to Molly and gave her the trophy. "Here, this is yours," she said to Molly.

"Why?" asked Molly. "You won the race, didn't you?"

"Lazy Gator did cross the finish line first," said Rocky, "but she didn't win. She was the one who changed the sign."

"I felt bad about it after the race," Lazy said. "So I told the judges what happened."

"All the skaters voted to make you the winner, Molly," Tabby said. "You are the nicest and most helpful skater of all."

Molly couldn't believe it. She had come in last, and she had still won the race!

Glossary

curb   [kurb] a raised border of stone along the side of a street

dizzy   [DIH zee] a feeling of spinning

famous   [FAY mus] very well known

fountain   [FOWN tun] a stream of water, or a statue made to shoot a stream of water

parade   [puh RAYD] many people marching

trophy   [TROH fee] a silver or gold metal cup or statue given to the winner of a contest

tuba   [TOO buh] a large musical instrument made of brass that makes a loud, deep sound

wobbled   [WAH buld] moved from side to side in an unsteady way